Old UPLAWMOOR

by

Uplawmoor Local Studies Group

Knockmade House on a summer's day in the early 1940s. The house was built by Robert Hardie and the baby in the pram in the picture is Patricia Erskine, who was born at Knockmade. When Pat's parents moved to Mid Uplaw in 1945 the house was sold to Charlie and Jessie Brown, her aunt and uncle. Jessie Brown was a local Guide captain.

© Uplawmoor Local Studies Group 2004
First published in the United Kingdom, 2004,
by Stenlake Publishing Ltd.
Telephone: 01290 551122
Printed by Cordfall Ltd., Glasgow, G21 2QA

ISBN 1 84033 321 9

The publishers regret that they cannot supply copies of any pictures featured in this book.

Taken during the experimental year of clock change in the winter of 1974/5, this photograph shows 'Papa' Ramage helping his grandsons Gordon and Zander McIlwham across the road. Scottish children went to school in darkness during this trial, and public and parental opinion ensured that the change did not become permanent. Recently the Westminster government has begun talks again about clock changes, as undoubtedly business with Europe from London would be aided by both parts of the continent having their clocks set to the same time, but the outcome of this for schoolchildren north of the Watford Gap would nonetheless be detrimental.

INTRODUCTION

The village of Uplawmoor perches on the wooded southern lip of the Neilston Gap, a valley that slices into the high ground of East Renfrewshire. At the foot of the valley lies Loch Libo, a small freshwater loch, which along with the adjacent marshy area is a Site of Special Scientific Interest and a Scottish Wildlife Trust reserve on account of the varied and rare aquatic plant life. The Lugton Water flows south-west from the loch, meandering through the fertile lowlands of Ayrshire and joining other bigger streams that enter the Firth of Clyde at Irvine. The upside of the situation of the village is the open views to the firth and the dramatic mountainous profile of Arran; the downside is the exposure to the moisture-laden winds from the south-west.

The history of Uplawmoor is intertwined with that of the Barony of Caldwell, which lay partly in the Parish of Neilston and partly in that of Beith. From the late thirteenth to the early twentieth century the lands of Caldwell belonged to the Mure family, who, despite their local importance, were rarely big players on the national stage.

William Mure was involved in the 'Pentland Rising' of 1666, and despite the fact that he and the tenants he had mustered at Shutterflat arrived too late to take part in the rout at Rullion Green, he was arrested later as an insurgent. Sprung by his wife from Dumbarton Castle where he was imprisoned, he escaped to Ireland then made his way into exile in the Low Countries. The Barony of Caldwell was forfeited to the Crown and given into the keeping of General Thomas Dalyell. Through the efforts of Lady Mure, who was imprisoned for a time with her daughters in Blackness Castle for her part in William's escape, the barony was eventually restored to the Mure family.

About a century later a Laird of Caldwell became a Baron of Exchequer, one of an elite group who administered Scotland after the Union. Although he had a house in Edinburgh and attended sittings of Parliament in Westminster, he maintained a close interest in the changes and developments in agriculture during his lifetime and implemented many of the improvements at Caldwell. Much of the woodland and many of the beech trees that he had planted along the roadways still flourish, but regrettably, Caldwell House, designed by Robert Adam, is currently a fire-gutted shell.

While the collected family papers of the Mures – the Caldwell Papers – are the main source of information about the area, old maps also provide vital information. In the map made by Timothy Pont in the 1590s the name 'Wowpla' occurs roughly in the position of South Uplaw Farm (most probably a multiple-tenancy fermtoun at that time). The name 'Knowglas' is given to the fermtoun closest to Loch Libo. The first real evidence of a small village on the present site comes from the poll tax rolls of 1696 when there were a few families living in cottages at Neukfoot, some of whom were engaged in handloom weaving. Although the economy of the area was firmly based on agriculture, there were a few small-scale industries. In the last quarter of the eighteenth century coal was mined on the slopes above Loch Libo with ingaun'es ('ingoing eyes' or shallow-sloping drift mines) driven into the hillside. Sand and gravel were extracted from natural mounds to the north-east of the loch. There was a tile works manufacturing the clay drainage tiles that were so necessary for the improvement of local farmland. In more recent times there was a sawmill.

The expansion of the village from its small core at Neukfoot accelerated with the opening in 1820 of the Paisley to Irvine turnpike road (now the A736) which ran through the Neilston Gap. In 1873 a parallel route was chosen for the railway line built by the Glasgow & South Western Railway which connected Glasgow, Barrhead and Neilston with Kilmarnock. The Mure family's aim of creating an estate village on a grandiose scale with large houses set in spacious gardens faltered after the building of two houses fronting the road and overlooking the loch, but what they began others continued. The railway made it possible for successful businessmen to live in Uplawmoor and work in Glasgow, and they built houses alongside the cottages of the agricultural workers.

Just over a century ago, the growth of the population justified the creation of the *quoad sacra* Parish of Caldwell, and the village got its own church. At around the same time Lady Georgiana Mure gifted a village hall, Caldwell Golf Club was formed, and as well as an inn, Uplawmoor had a school, post office, bank and some shops. In 1903 it acquired a second railway station when a line was built by the Caledonian Railway from Glasgow to Ardrossan. Following the arrival of the motor car a garage was established in Uplawmoor.

Very few of these services remain in the twenty-first century, although the village school is thriving, as is the former inn (now Uplawmoor Hotel) and the golf club, while the Mure Hall has recently been upgraded and extended through the efforts of the community. The church continues to be valued by its members, and like the Mure Hall the church hall is used by a variety of organisations. But there are no shops, no post office, no garage, no bank and no stations. In spite of the lack of services, the sense of identity remains. Village activities such as the 'Gala' and the 'Gardens Open Days' are well-supported, and Uplawmoor is still a good place to live.

Irene Hughson

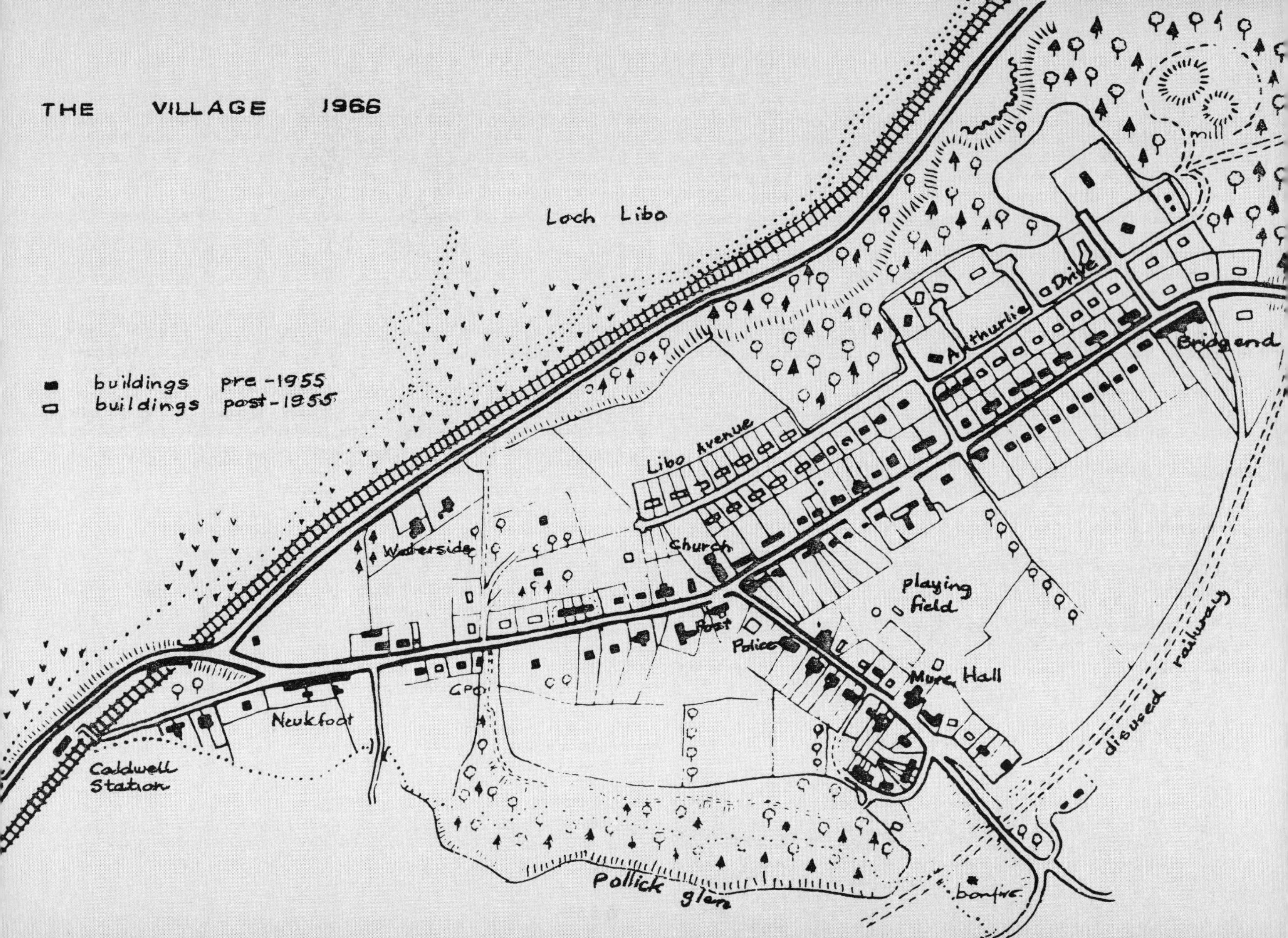

THE VILLAGE 1966
Loch Libo
buildings pre-1955
buildings post-1955
Arthurlie Drive
Bridgend
Libo Avenue
Waterside
Church
playing field
Post
Police
Mure Hall
GPO
Neukfoot
disused railway
Caldwell Station
Pollick glen
bonfire
mill

Caldwell Tower is situated above the valley of the Lugton Water on a small hill that forms part of Old Barn Farm, owned by David King. The tower is probably of sixteenth century origin, and is thought to stand on the site of the medieval Castle of Caldwell. John Mure, Laird of Caldwell, is recorded as being involved in a bloody feudal battle in the district in 1543 known as the 'Field of the Muir of Glasgow'. On 27 March 1549 he was indicted for having 'with his fyve brothers and twenty-six others, armed in warlike manner invaded Robert Master of Semphill and his servands for their slauchter, near the place and tour [tower] of Cauldwell, and put them to flight'. Mure and his brothers were granted a remission for their share in this adventure by the Crown In 1553. In 1651 it is recorded that 'Inglismen' broke the gate of Caldwell Tower, leading to the following account entry: 'Item for mending ye lock of the tour gaitt of Cauldwell, and for naills yrto, quich the Inglismen brak in May 1651 – 0.14.0 [fourteen shillings]'. The original building was allowed to fall into disrepair when it was forfeited in 1666 and given to General Tam Dalyell of the Binns. Certain surviving stones bear mouldings, which could be part of the original castle, and the arched gateway at Hall of Caldwell was recovered from this site. The tower, a scheduled ancient monument, still stands, and there has been interest in converting it into a home.

In 1773 Baron Mure (Baron of Exchequer in Scotland, 1761, and Lord Rector of Glasgow University, 1764–5) commissioned Robert Adam to design 'a mansionhouse with a castle air' befitting his social position. In a letter to his client, Adam wrote: 'The lottery goes on most swimmingly, and I am very much obliged to you for giving it an opportunity … of rewarding your good offices with a 40 or 50,000 pound prize. I am bound by that most powerful motive, self-interest, to wish you success, as I do believe that either of the above sums would soon realize [sic] our ideas at Caldwell; and I flatter myself, when that happens, there will be few so good houses of the size in Scotland, and none so convenient'. Despite this obsequious yet arrogant reply, Robert Adam took some years to begin designing a house for Baron Mure. In a later letter he informed his client that he and his brother were facing bankruptcy, suggesting that a 'valuation' or financial reference could help their situation. This seems to have been forthcoming, clearing the way for work to continue. Caldwell House was duly built, but by the latter part of the nineteenth century, estate duties and heavy taxation meant that the house had been let to a prominent businessman. It was sold to Glasgow Corporation in 1920 and used as a home for children with learning difficulties. Having been severely damaged by fire in 1995, it is now in a state of dilapidation.

In 1715 William Mure, advocate, built a hall house on the Caldwell Estate about half a mile south-west of his ancestral home, the old Castle of Caldwell. Called Hall of Caldwell, this remained in the Mure family until the 1930s. The last of the line to live there was Colonel William Mure, with his wife Georgiana and their children William (b.1898) and Marjorie Janet (b.1896). On the colonel's return from the Boer War in 1902 he developed and extended the Hall, as well as carrying out extensive tree-planting across the parish. He intended to make Uplawmoor a model 'Garden Village', with Pollick Glen a distinctive feature, but his ambitious plans were never fully realised. The church in Uplawmoor was largely built through the influence of Colonel William Mure, who also donated two stained glass windows to Dunlop Parish Church. He lived at the Hall until his death, aged 42, of appendicitis in 1912, and was survived by his wife and two children. According to a contemporary report in the *Kilmarnock Standard*, his funeral was 'one of the largest and most impressive that had been seen in the West of Scotland'. The cortege travelled from the Hall to Neilston, with the colonel's coffin 'borne upon a hay cart lined with moss taken from the Caldwell Estate, and drawn by five powerful Clydesdale horses'. Having been divided into two residences, Hall of Caldwell is still occupied. The arched gateway from the old Castle of Caldwell has been built into the garden wall of the Hall and can be seen facing the crossroads of the B775 and B776.

This nostalgic view of Uplawmoor looks towards the centre of the village – where the older houses and church are located – from the east. House-building during the twentieth century gradually extended Uplawmoor eastwards along the Neilston road (right), and also southwards towards Uplawmoor station (left). On 31 March 1962 the station was closed, and the double track line, which had previously extended to Ardrossan, was lifted as far as Neilston, three and a half miles away. A busy commuter service still operates between Glasgow and Neilston, where trains now terminate. Uplawmoor station was used as a peaceful overnight resting place for Queen Elizabeth, the late Queen Mother, when she visited Scotland in the royal train in early 1964. The corn stooks in the foreground are in the lower meadow of East Uplaw Farm and date from an era of arable, grazing and dairy farming, now replaced in this area of East Renfrewshire by specialist farming such as the rearing of cattle and sheep and the production of silage. Today East Uplaw is a dairy farm managed on an all-organic basis, and since the introduction of organic farming skylarks are reported to be heard once again.

This picture shows the thatched cottage at Neukfoot which in 1910 was the location of the village post office. Having been modernised the cottage still stands. The house to the left of it (out of shot in this picture) still has its original cruck roof.

This view of the village from the north dates from the beginning of the twentieth century. The houses still remain but have been supplemented by new buildings.

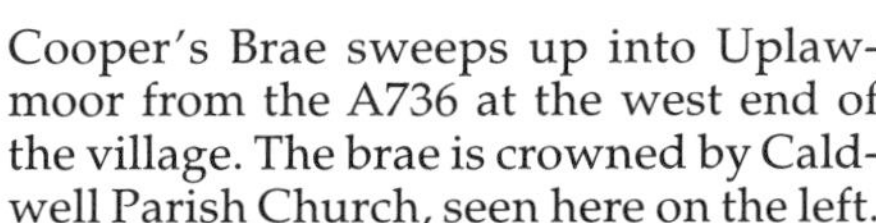

Cooper's Brae sweeps up into Uplawmoor from the A736 at the west end of the village. The brae is crowned by Caldwell Parish Church, seen here on the left.

Caldwell Church doesn't have a steeple, so this view of Tannoch Road is misleadingly captioned 'Uplawmoor from the Church Steeple'. Instead the photograph was probably taken from a window high up in the church's gable. Uplawmoor station, on the Glasgow to Ardrossan line, lay on the edge of the village to the south of Tannoch Road (out of shot to the left in this picture).

Crossgates stands in a commanding position opposite the church in Uplawmoor. It was once a single-storey estate cottage with yew trees standing in front of it, and when the upper storey was built access was by an iron stair. The building became the first police station in the village and in 1923 Uplawmoor's first telephone was installed there. This photograph was taken in the winter of 1951/52. The lady on the left is Mrs Shearer, who lived in Crossgates, which by this time had ceased to be the police station and had been converted into a single dwelling. Mr Shearer worked as a signalman on the Glasgow to Kilmarnock railway line. The lady on the right is Cathy Gemmell. She and her husband were newly returned from Montevideo, and because of the severe shortage of housing after the war were lodging with Mrs Shearer.

The Lynn Waterfall is near the head of the Glen, a wooded valley and popular beauty spot where many people exercise their dogs and go for walks. Called the Water of Lynn, the burn that feeds the waterfall flows from the peat marshes under the shadow of nearby Knockmade Hill to the south, then across undulating farmland to the dense tree-covered area of woodland of the Glen, situated within the village. Near the top of the Glen the burn flows into a deep valley from where it continues down a ravine whose slopes become increasingly steep. This ravine is known by some older villagers as the Dead Man's Gulch. The Glen and Water of Lynn form part of the county boundary between East Renfrewshire and North Ayrshire. The man standing on the southern bank of the burn in this photograph is Parker Dale, brother of Jean Dale who owned a grocer's shop on Neilston Road in the village.

The Glen was privately owned by Miss Allan who lived in a cottage on its northern edge in a house called Beechbrae facing Neilston Road. Her first name was Christina but she was always known as Miss Allan, even by her close friends. Her early years had been spent in Tarbert Loch Fyne where her father, an excise officer, was based. Miss Allan reputedly bought the Glen 'instead of a fur coat', and from the outset wanted it to be used and enjoyed by members of the public. She was a keen gardener, planting the trees around Beechbrae and laying out the extensive garden

– which included a badminton court – herself. Miss Allan was a lady of many interests who travelled widely, including visiting Russia twice at a time when relations with that country weren't particularly friendly. A respected and successful optician, she became a partner in the once well-known Glasgow firm of Trotters. She lived a long and active life, and on one occasion was witnessed playing badminton in her eighties with a gentleman of similar years. After her death in August 1965 the Glen was inherited by Primrose Orr, a close neighbour from across Neilston Road. Mrs Orr then donated it to Renfrew District Council (now East Renfrewshire Council) to maintain its upkeep and preserve it for the enjoyment of the public. Three large houses have since been built on the extensive grounds around Beechbrae.

In the 1920s Pollick Cottage was both the home and workshop of a shoemaker and a branch of the National Bank of Scotland. According to the notice outside, the latter was open between 9.30 and 2 on Tuesdays and Thursdays. When Alan Craig retired here from Finniebrae Farm he renamed the cottage Finniebrae. It retains its rural appearance today, despite extensive renovation during the 1980s, the most radical element of which involved the resiting of the front door in the left side elevation.

This grocer's shop was built in 1934 by Parker Dale, who emigrated to Australia in the late 1930s. His sister Jean, who took it over and ran it until 1972, had previously trained at the 'Dough School' (the colloquial name for the Glasgow & West of Scotland College of Domestic Science), and also managed the kitchens at Hawkhead Hospital. Many villagers remember Priscilla the goat who grazed behind the shop, and was a favourite sight in the village, especially when being taken out for a walk. This was one of three shops in the village, the others being a post office which occupied a number of different sites over the years, and a general store and newsagents at Neukfoot. In 1972 Jean Dale's shop became a gift shop owned by Marion Grant. It was demolished in 1976 and the house at 62 Neilston Road built on the site.

Taken in 1973, these rear views of Bridgend show how the property was once divided into five houses. There were two at each end, with access to the upper flats by way of external stairs, and one in the centre which was two-storied. Now a single dwelling, Bridgend fronts Neilston Road and stands at the entrance to Bridgend Walk, leading to the Castburn Path. This is the lane which winds its way south of Neilston Road before emerging on Tannoch Road. Following the old railway line, it overlooks peaceful farmland, and being free of traffic is a favourite walk for young and old.

Opposite: This pre-1915 photograph was taken at Smiddyhill Farm. Uplawmoor's rural setting meant that the songs of larks, thrushes, corncrakes and curlews were once commonly heard, along with owls at night and the distinctive call of the cuckoo. Changes in farming practices mean that less birdsong is now noticeable in the area.

Occupying a central location in the village on Neilston Road at the junction with Tannoch Road, Caldwell Church (with manse attached) was opened in 1889. It was built by William Stewart of Barrhead, a direct descendant of whom lives in Uplawmoor. William Ingram of Glasgow was the architect and the Revd David Stewart the first minister. The Hon. Mrs Mure of Caldwell was active in raising funds to build the church, as was William Mure, the young laird, and support was given by other local worthies such as Dr Pride of Neilston, Mrs Glen of Carlibar and Alexander Crum of Thornliebank. Since 1889 only six ministers have served in Uplawmoor: David Stewart, John Irvine Fortescue, John Gunn, Edwin Lowe, John Cubie, and John Campbell. A new manse has since been built behind the church and the old one converted into meeting rooms and a small hall. Today the church maintains a spiritual focal point within the village, with an active Sunday Club (formerly the Sunday school), a Boys' Brigade company, as well as a Friday Lunch Club during the winter months. A vintage motorcycle club (originally established by Willie Bates of Glenhead) uses the church hall (and car park), as do many local charitable groups, among them those supporting Save the Children, Multiple Sclerosis, Accord and Macmillan Cancer Relief. In 2004 ramps and toilets for the disabled were installed.

Opposite: John Killawee, a ploughman from Ireland, poses with his two horses, Billy (left) and Volunteer. He was one of two men employed on the Fulton family farm of Smiddyhill. In the early decades of the twentieth century a local teacher encouraged schoolchildren to anglicize the farm's name to Smithyhill, but the original Scots name prevailed on Ordnance Survey maps. Farmland was still occasionally ploughed by horses until the late 1960s, although by then the tractor had taken over at most farms. Robert Fulton's family farmed Smiddyhill from 1900, and his descendants still own the land. The farm itself is much older, with the date 1791 recorded on the wall of the barn, and now houses four families in up-to-date homes – a modern fermtoun.

Haymaking at Mid Uplaw Farm.

This photograph of Margaret Carswell was taken at Mid Uplaw Farm in 1920. Margaret was the grandmother of the farm's present owner, Patricia Erskine, and Jen MacLeod of East Uplaw Farm, and was also a founder member of the Uplawmoor branch of the Scottish Women's Rural Institute. She lived in the area for 85 years, and saw both the first and last trains to use the Glasgow to Ardrossan railway line, which her husband William helped to build. The Uplawmoor sign was rescued by Bill Frew when the station closed and some of the letters from it were used to make a nameplate for Mid Uplaw Farm which can still be seen today.

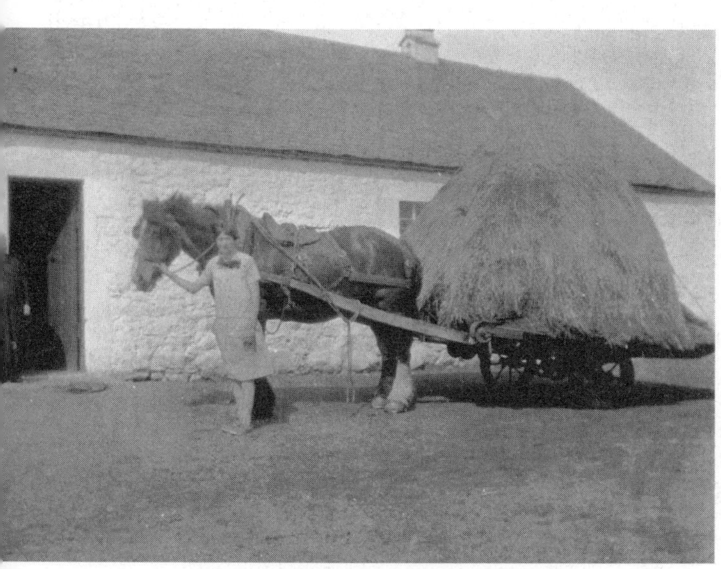

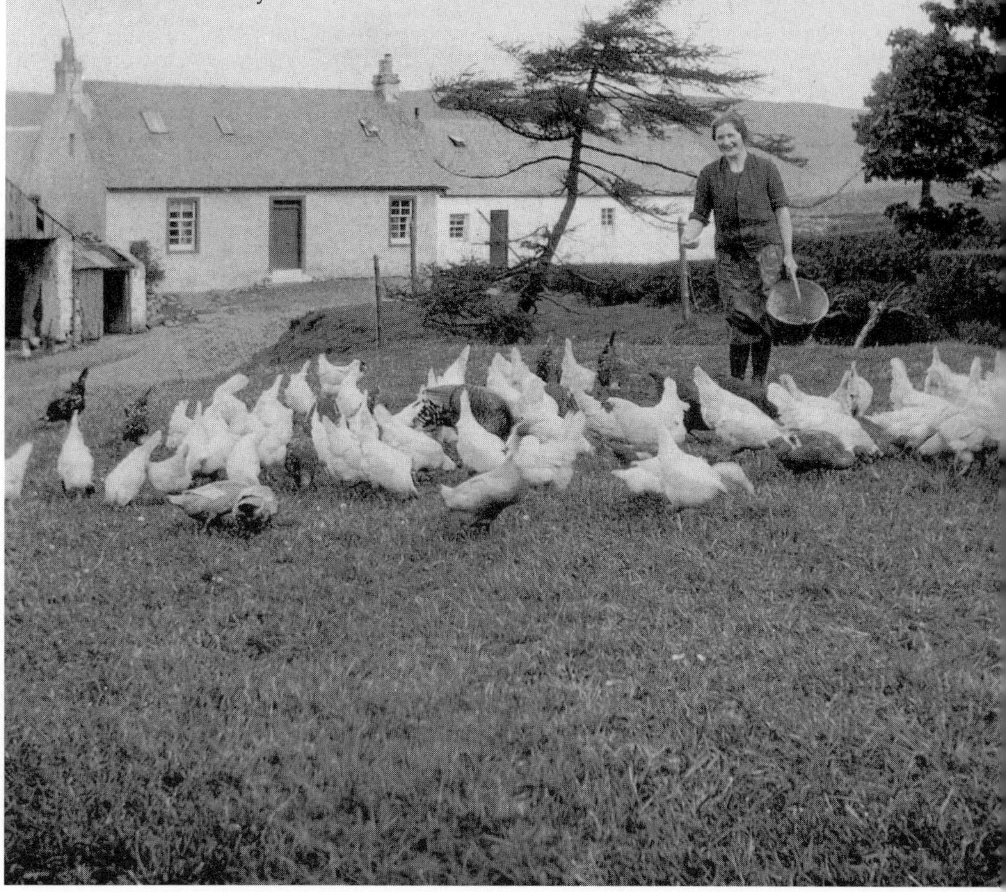

Robert and Jane Frew, the grandparents of Patricia Erskine (née Frew), outside Muirhouse Farm.

A maid photographed at Smiddyhill Farm with an Ayrshire cow in the days when it was still the norm for cattle to have horns. Nowadays Highland cattle are the only breed that are commonly seen with horns, as it became normal practice to de-horn cows after the Second World War. This was often done by sawing the horns off adult beasts, a practice that occasionally caused distress to the animal. Today newly born calves are debudded by cauterisation before any horn growth takes place. The practice was introduced as cows in a herd often harmed each other, or indeed the herdsman, and can still be seen butting each other, but with little likelihood of causing injury. Horns did not always grow naturally into elegant curving pairs and farmers who showed their cattle often rigged up a pulley system above the byre stall, with weights, which when attached to the growing horns encouraged attractive curvature.

Crumyards Farm is situated halfway between Uplawmoor and Neilston, and had a typical stackyard (complete with hens) of the sort described in *Reminiscences of a Country Doctor, 1840–1914,* by Dr David Pride of Neilston. In his book he describes 'an incident in natural history sufficiently notable in the development of the flying machine' which occurred at Crumyards Farm on 3 August 1911. On that day two aeroplanes flown by James Valentine and Gustav Hamel on a prize flight from Edinburgh passed comparatively low over the farm, meaning that the beating of the propellors could be heard distinctly. The noise didn't disturb the hens, which continued rooting about in the stackyard, but the moment the fowls beheld the gigantic bird-like forms above them they were considerably alarmed, screeching and rushing headlong to shelter beneath sheds, carts and hedgerows. Following the noise and sighting absolute calm ensued for almost thirty minutes before any hens were seen or heard. Gustav Hamel flew the first consignment of airmail in Britain on 9 September 1911 and both he and James Valentine were members of the British team competing in races for the Gordon Bennett Cup in the early years of the twentieth century.

Opposite: The origins of the Mure Hall are unclear, but the original building is associated with the village's first school. An early schoolroom was in existence by 1857, located within Glenhead Cottage, and the first hall is thought to have been adjacent to it. In 1912 the hall/school was enlarged as a tribute to William Mure, with the addition of two small rooms to the front of the existing schoolroom. The following year Lady Georgiana Mure gifted the hall to the village, when it was administered by a committee of eight and a number of trustees. In 1939 the building was officially entitled the Mure Memorial Hall, and in 1952 it was extended and a stage built in the area of the original schoolroom. The 20th Laird of Caldwell, William Mure, visited the hall in 1965 and expressed concern at its need for redecoration, offering to match, pound for pound, any sum collected by Uplawmoor residents. The following year the building was taken over by Renfrew District Council, which extended it in 1968 to improve kitchen and toilet facilities. The Mure Hall Company was formed in 2001 to refurbish and extend the building, which is leased from East Renfrewshire Council. A lottery grant was secured, and along with financial help from the council plus fund-raising among villagers the necessary sums were raised to carry out the work. On 26 April 2002 the extended and refurbished hall was officially opened.

The Uplawmoor Hotel (formerly 'the Inn') dates from the stagecoach era of the eighteenth century. Its traditional character survives to this day, largely as a result of the efforts of Ian and Josie Smith, who ran it for thirteen years following the Second World War. In the 1960s an extension in a style reminiscent of Charles Rennie Mackintosh was designed by James Gray, village resident, who was an architect for the electricity board. Wood rafters, colourful hunting scenes and a fine collection of horse brasses, pistols, tankards and harness contribute to an atmosphere of warmth and comfort, fostered by the current owners, Stuart and Emma Peacock. The inn is the focus for many village activities, including meetings of the Ouplaymuir Burns Club, so-named because it is believed that this is how the village's name was spelt during the period that Burns was writing his works. The club was founded in 1840 with John Glen as president and twelve members. Numbers have increased since those early days and the annual Burns Supper is always well supported with lots of home-grown talent to the fore. The Burns Club generously organises art and essay competitions in the primary school, and the singing and poetry event is one of the highlights of the school year. The Bridge Club, which used to meet in the hotel, now uses the Mure Hall, but many village organisations meet informally in the public bar to this day, while on occasion community council meetings end up in the hotel too. Up to 600 meals are served each week in the hotel, and the Sunday night quiz, a recent innovation, is a great success.

Uplawmoor School opened in 1877 following the passing of the 1872 Education Act (Scotland), which made schooling compulsory for children aged five to thirteen. Electricity was installed in 1928, a telephone in 1946, and coal-fired heating was replaced by storage heaters in 1957. In 1919 a plate of soup could be bought at lunchtime during the summer months for a ha'penny; cocoa was offered in the winter. A formal school meals service was introduced in 1946. There was brief upheaval during the Second World War when evacuee children arrived in 1939, returning to their homes the following year. A glass-fronted bookcase in the headmaster's room marked the beginning of the building's use as a library, a role it was given over to when the school relocated to new premises in Tannoch Road in 1968. Other parts of the former school were used by a variety of organisations, with the West of Scotland Vintage Motorcycle Club meeting there on Monday evenings for many years. After temporary moves to the Mure Hall and the church vestry, Uplawmoor Library is once more located within the Mure Hall, following the latter's enlargement and renovation. Today the former school, now a listed building, is occupied as two houses having undergone restoration to its stonework. The three trees planted in 1937 to mark the Coronation of George VI still stand.

An end of term party taking place in June 1929 in the garden of the schoolhouse, organised by Mrs Forbes, whose husband was headmaster from 1924 to 1937 and can be seen in the centre background. The former school playground and part of the garden illustrated here are now the site of a number of cottage-type homes built for local retired people and given the name Mure Place. The fan dancers include Nancy Frew (who now occupies a house on this site), Helen Goodman, Mattie Houston, Janet King, Jean Andrew and Jean Clark.

Mr Forbes, headmaster of Uplawmoor School, photographed in June 1929 in the garden of the schoolhouse with the school's entire roll.

This group of pupils from Uplawmoor School was photographed in 1935.
Back row: David Ralston, Willie Stirling, Jack Lawns, Jacky Raeside.
Front row: Margaret Richardson, Jessie Richardson, Morag Campbell, Mary Kirk, Jean Campbell, Isa Andrew, Maggie and Jessie Buchanan (twins), Netta Lawns.
David Ralston was killed during the Second World War whilst serving with the RAF, and Jack Lawns also died during the war, in Burma.

Prior to the Second World War boys at Uplawmoor School grew potatoes and other vegetables within the school's premises as part of their education. The area shown is where Nos. 1–8 Mure Place were built in 1972. The wall in the background still stands, and the houses of Libo Avenue, behind it, were constructed in 1960–61 by Leggatt of Barrhead, a firm which also built many other houses in the village.

Dating from November 1966, this is one of the last photographs to be taken at the old school in Neilston Road, and shows head teacher Robert Brown with teachers Jessie Baird (left, née Matthews) and Christine Thom.

Back row: Carole McCallum, Angela and Rosemary Wright, Helen Fisher, Rhona McPhun, Shona Middleton, Fiona McGregor, Amanda Simonsen, Mandy Grant

Middle row: Brian Addie, Alan Fulton, Alan Paton, David King, Ian MacLeod, George Cartwright, Alexander Inglis, Graham Gold, Gordon Walker, David Pollok

Front row: Kathryn Richards, Fiona Munro, Jacqueline McCallum, Pippa Coates, Martha King, Lorna McKie, Judith Harkness, Fiona Simpson, Lynn Turner

(Tom Thomson was absent)

Dating from 1968, this was the first school photograph to be taken at the new school in Tannoch Road and shows the entire complement of pupils and teachers at the time.

Staff: Robert Brown, head teacher; Mrs Laws, student; Mrs Gunn; Mrs Thom; Mrs Mackay, secretary; Mrs Baird

Fifth row: Ewan Robertson, David Welsh, Ian McCallum, Duncan Welsh, Timothy Heath, John Murray, Keith Walker, Graham Watson, Tony Williams, David Murray, Douglas Currie, Ian Rundle, Douglas Scott, Ian Walker, Alexander Inglis

Fourth row: Alison Irwin, Carole McCallum, Helen Fisher, Shona Middleton, Rona McPhun, Rhona Cunningham, Dianne Addie, Sheena McPhun, Christine McDonald, Pauline Vallance, Helen Richardson, Mary Kerr, Fiona McGregor, Rosie and Angie Wright

Third row: Fifi Warnock, Eileen Allan, Susan Hutchison, Murray Pollok, Brian Addie, Christopher Moorhouse, Scott McCallum, Alan Paton, Campbell Erskine, Gordon Walker, Nicholas Fry, Ian MacLeod, David Pollok, unknown, Eric Richards, Alan Fulton, Elspeth Inglis, Gillian Adam, Audrey Scott

Second row: Martha King, Fiona Simpson, Judith Harkness, Jackie McCallum, Susan Ramsay, Euan Addie, Brendan Smith, Graham Gold, Martin Kerr, Colin McGregor, David King, Isobel McDonald, Mandy Grant, Jill McCallum, Lorna McKie, Alison Welsh, Lynn Turner

Front row: Kerr Anderson, Stuart Pollok, Andrew Niven, Alison Scott, Morna Simpson, Susan Guthrie, Una Munro, Libby Ramsay, Helen McGregor, Lindsay Dunlop, Gillian Robertson, Claire Wright, Kathryn Richards, Morag Inglis, Sarah-Jane Cairns-Smith, Elizabeth Ann Gold, Neil MacLeod, Scott McCallum, Steven Morris

This pre-Second World War photograph shows Caldwell Garage, which was situated at the junction of the main (A736) Barrhead to Irvine road and Neilston Road. Part of the parapet of the bridge carrying the main road over the Glasgow–Kilmarnock railway is visible in the left foreground. In the background to the right are the cottages at Neukfoot where weavers once lived, and where in more recent times the village post office and shop were located. Near the foot of the hill, on the left-hand side, was a house which had stables for horses employed in assisting heavy carts up the hill into the village. Caldwell Garage was owned by Johnny Gemmill, who acted as chauffeur to Colonel Mure and also looked after the Caldwell Estate vehicles. Johnny bought the garage after serving in the RAF during the Second World War and lived in one of the cottages at Neukfoot before moving to The Firs by Caldwell Tower. The garage was also the base for the local taxi service, for which Johnny was the driver. In addition to carrying out repairs, servicing cars and dispensing petrol, Johnny Gemmill also fixed local children's bicycles free of charge, dispensing road safety advice as he did so. In the early 1970s the site was taken over by Welsh's Garages, a firm specialising not in motor repairs but the building of garages. It is still used by the firm today, and they now also make porches and conservatories, as well as undertaking general building work.

Uplawmoor was once served by two railway companies; indeed the expansion of the village would not have taken place had it not been for the railways. The oldest line is that which runs parallel to the A736 to the north of the village. It was built as the Glasgow, Barrhead & Kilmarnock Railway, reaching Uplawmoor – where the station was called Caldwell – in 1873. As well as providing transport for Uplawmoor residents who worked and shopped in Glasgow and Kilmarnock, it was a useful link for golfers travelling to Caldwell Golf Club – an important factor in the early development of the club. Although the line is still operational with regular passenger services between Glasgow, Kilmarnock, Dumfries and Carlisle, Caldwell station (renamed Caldwell for Uplawmoor in 1962) closed on 7 November 1966.

In 1901 the Caledonian Railway began construction of the Lanarkshire & Ayrshire Railway linking Lugton and Cathcart via Neilston High and Uplawmoor. Uplawmoor station opened on this line in 1903. It was to the south of the village at the end of Tannoch Road. Services ran from Glasgow Central and the line was used in the summer by trippers travelling to Ardrossan and Saltcoats, making it particularly important as a link to the Arran steamers at Ardrossan harbour. Local passenger services beyond Uplawmoor ceased in 1932, although trains between Glasgow and the village continued to offer an important commuter service until 31 March 1962.

Taken *c.*1920, this photograph shows Nos. 1 and 2 Station Cottages, now 27 and 29 Tannoch Road. The children standing on the pathway are Peg and Jean Andrew, daughters of John Andrew who was employed by the railway. John was killed on the line when an unscheduled train ran him down. His son, Willie Andrew, lived at 1 Station Cottages until 1997. At one time the Andrews had a pet parrot which could imitate a train's whistle and made people approaching the station run, thinking they were going to miss their departure.

Three individuals are named in this photograph, taken at Uplawmoor station. James Raeside was booking clerk at the station from 3 March 1909 to 10 May 1913; Mr Lockhart was the first stationmaster; while the little girl on the left is Jessie Lockhart (1904–1975), who was born in the stationmaster's house and educated at the village school. Her son, Ken Steedman, lives in Neilston Road.

AG 5195 was a Tilling–Stevens bus bought new by the Scottish Transport Co. of Kilmarnock in 1930. It was typical of the fleet of red buses which served the village of Uplawmoor during the 1930s, operating between Glasgow and Kilmarnock via Barrhead, Neilston, Uplawmoor, Caldwell, Lugton, Dunlop and Stewarton. This service was commenced by Scottish Transport (Western SMT from 1932 onwards) in the mid-1920s and provided links which are almost non-existent today. Until quite recently older inhabitants of the village continued to describe their bus service as simply 'the Transport', a reminder of days long-gone. *Picture courtesy of Robert Grieves.*

Loch Libo is a natural loch situated in a narrow valley below Uplawmoor that forms the westward continuation of the Neilston Gap. The loch is separated from the village by a busy railway line and the A736 road between Glasgow and the Clyde Coast at Irvine. The water and its surrounding woods and wetlands form a nature reserve under the care of the Scottish Wildlife Trust. Pike fishing is carried out by members of a club. Anyone viewing the loch and its sylvan setting today would find difficulty in believing that it was once a busy mining area. In the later years of the eighteenth century and early nineteenth century numerous small coal mines were worked around the loch and in the hillside immediately above it to the south-east. Overzealous mining close to and under the loch led to a disaster in 1792, when eight miners were drowned in a sudden inrush of water. Another mine at the south-west end of the loch suddenly flooded in 1833, but fortunately the miners below ground just managed to get clear. Commercial mining ceased in the 1840s and nature has now covered any evidence of industrial activity above ground.

Before the climate changes of the later years of the twentieth century, curling was a popular activity on Loch Libo during suitably hard winter frosts (the last grand match took place on the loch in 1974). Established in 1869, Uplawmoor Curling Club initially held its meetings at the Inn, and also occasionally curled on the Caplaw Dam at Peesweep when the ice was thick enough (a layer of at least four inches was required). There were evening sessions by lantern, with whisky galore and a great time had by all. Both these locations were used until curling was established in 1979 at the artificial rink at Greenacres on the Howwood Road. Complete club records have been kept since 1895, when gold and silver medals presented by Colonel William Mure were first awarded. The medal-winners board was formerly located in a small room at the Inn, but following the building's renovation the board was moved to Greenacres. A club badge was designed in 1964 by Mrs S. Simpson and is the emblem used on the jerseys worn by club members.

The tiny hamlet of Shilford (now officially spelt Shillford) lies within the Neilston Gap on the watershed between the Cowden Burn, which flows eastwards to join the Levern, and the Thorter Burn, which flows westwards into Loch Libo. Situated on the turnpike road between Paisley and Irvine, it had a tollhouse and boasted a mill and a smiddy. It was a busy place with roads leading from it to Neilston, Uplawmoor and the Braes. There were once railway workers' houses in the narrow strip of land between the road and the railway. Although these have disappeared, the smiddy has become a petrol station and shop, the area once occupied by the mill has become a bus garage, and there are agricultural engineering premises too.

This picnic scene, taken in 1968, shows Miss Halley with Alan and Gordon Paton and David, Murray and Stuart Pollok on the Castburn Path, also known as the 'right of way' or Cinder Path. Following the opening of Uplawmoor station in 1903 it provided a route from the east end of the village to the station, and as a result of the railway's construction had to be realigned to lie alongside the track. It is one of the few legally registered rights of way in East Renfrewshire, and was upgraded by Renfrew District Council and Sustrans in the 1980s with the active support of Uplawmoor Community Council, which acquired the land it occupies from a local farmer and Caldwell Estates.

Caldwell Golf Club was founded in 1903 and laid out on land rented from William Mure of Caldwell. It was opened by Provost John Shanks of Barrhead. The land was purchased in 1924 at a cost of £4,000, raised through the issue of debentures. Today the club has a membership in excess of 600, a far cry from the fourteen members at its opening. Its course was laid out by golf professional Willie Fernie of Troon, who was the Open champion at Musselburgh in 1883 and a relative of Claire Orr of Bogside, a well-loved resident of the village. This 1922 photograph shows assistant greenkeeper Jim Raeside mowing the grass next to the clubhouse.

In 1928 the golf course was altered using plans drawn up by the famous course architect James Braid, five times Open champion. Further alterations were carried out in 1996 resulting in a standard scratch course score of 71, and more adjustments were made to the course in 2003 and 2004. Famous golfers who have competed on the course for the A. P. Scott Memorial Trophy include Sam Torrance, Bernard Gallacher, John McTear and Ronnie Shade. In Findlay Black and Heather Anderson the club is proud to have two amateurs who rose to achieve recognition with not only Scotland but also Great Britain and Ireland. This picture shows the clubhouse as it looked in the late 1930s.

This photograph shows, left to right: Charlie Brown, who was church organist and also centrally involved in organising all types of village events; David Carslaw, headmaster of the village school and winner of the Caldwell Golf Club championship this year (1952); Mr J. S. Deas, club secretary; and Ernest Gillespie, runner-up in the 1952 championship. Ernest worked as a draftsman for the well-known firm of Babcock & Wilcox and was awarded a commemorative certificate on completion of twenty-five years continuous service. He designed the house called Burnknock in Tannoch Road, which is still occupied by a member of his family, and is remembered as keeping bees. David Carslaw had been an English teacher at Eastwood High School before moving to Uplawmoor Primary as head teacher from 1950–56.

Uplawmoor Tennis Club was founded in 1964, when the first two courts were officially opened on 29 August by Mr Aikman Thompson, vice president of the West of Scotland Lawn Tennis Association. The National Playing Fields Association, Renfrew Second District Council and the Scottish Education Department all gave grants, but the bulk of the funding came from donations from villagers, founding members and local clubs. This photograph dates from finals day in 1967 and shows Elizabeth Scott; Alison Todd, ladies' champion; Jack Walker, president; Mrs Dow; John Pollok, gents champion; and Sandy McIlwham. The brick clubhouse behind the group was demolished in 2001 when changing rooms were provided in the refurbished and extended Mure Hall, which reopened in 2002.

When Elizabeth (Cissie) Montgomery married William (Willie) Fulton on 3 June 1933 the
wedding united neighbouring farming families from Crumyards and Smiddyhill. The
couple were married by Revd Robert Barr, who ministered at Neilston Parish Church
from 1895 to 1952. This photograph was taken in the garden of Crumyards Farm. The
bride was one of a family of ten, and her siblings were Ellen, Robert, Mary, Matthew, John,
Margaret, Janet, Catherine and William. Willie Fulton was one of nine, and his brothers
and sisters were named Annie, Mary, Janet, Jeannie, Ellen, Andrew, Margaret and Robert.

During the Second World War Uplawmoor and Neilston combined to form a company of the Home Guard and amongst those illustrated here are Jack Steel, Bob Borland and John Ferguson. The Home Guard was formed during the Second World War as a last line of defence against the very real threat of invasion after the fall of France. It was mainly composed of older men in the community and those in reserved occupations. Teenagers Jack Raeside and George Richardson, complete with tin hats and bicycles, acted as messengers for the local Home Guard.

This photograph of convalescing soldiers being greeted by Sir Harry Lauder is thought to have been taken at Hall of Caldwell during the Second World War. One of the men is wearing the uniform of the Royal Army Medical Corps, while others have on 'hospital blues', and some men appear to belong to the Polish Army. *Picture courtesy Evening Times/The Herald/ Sunday Herald.*

A photograph from the late 1920s of the Carswell boys from Mid Uplaw Farm. Behind them is the bridge over the former Glasgow to Ardrossan railway line at the eastern end of the village.

Robert Carswell pictured beside the Commore Dam on the Moyne Moor. Robert, who was brought up at Mid Uplaw Farm, became a science teacher.

This photograph was taken on Coronation Day, 1937, and shows headmaster Mr Forbes on the right with Maisie Dale, Jean Dale's sister-in-law, playing the bagpipes, and Revd John Fortescue (minister of Caldwell Church from 1925–1957) on the left. Guides and Scouts were amongst those who took part in the Coronation parade.

Called the Coons, this concert party was formed in the early 1950s to celebrate the Coronation of Queen Elizabeth II in 1953. Several village faces can be identified. Jack Steel is at the far left of the picture, with John Ferguson next in the line-up but standing behind him. Those in the back row include Tommy Bates, Bill Frew, Tommy Dick, David Carslaw (head teacher of the primary school), Charlie Brown, and Lawrence Inglis. Annie Bates is in the front row to the right of the lady draped in the Union flag, and Irene Allison is standing second from the right.

Fetes were held in Uplawmoor between 1948 and 1951 in a field halfway down the hill towards the 'low' (Caldwell) station, in order to raise funds for renovating the Mure Hall. The houses at 1, 3 and 5 Glen Lane (Cuillin, The Braes and Kintail Cottage) and 9A and 11 Neilston Road (Kinnoull and Haldon), now occupy the site of the field.

Uplawmoor Women's Rural Institute (WRI) was founded in 1922 with a hundred members. By 1953 this figure had reached 135, while in 1976 it had dropped to eighty-seven. In 2004 it stands at forty. Uplawmoor WRI won the George Outram Trophy in the Scottish Community Drama festival in May 1932, and although the drama group was later dissolved it then reformed as the Barrhead Players, which included men. The WRI have won many prizes at federation shows and in 1964 Meg Pollok won the Lena Meiklejohn Trophy for making and embroidering a dress. This photograph shows part of the celebrations for the WRI's golden jubilee in December 1972. The three standing ladies are (left to right) Mary Montgomery from Crumyards; Jessie Woodrow from Neukfoot Cottages, who ran one of the village shops; and Liz Buchanan who lived in Glenpark on Neilston Road. Sitting down, right to left, are Weilda Raeside, federation chairman; May Wilson, president; and Elizabeth Taylor from Cowdenmill Farm.

Margaret Hunter, Meg Pollok, David Riddet and Gerry Gray, members of Uplawmoor Community Council, examine images of Uplawmoor at a photographic exhibition in the Mure Hall on 12 April 1991. This was very well-attended and in response to high demand a follow-up day was arranged in the church hall to allow all the primary school children and teachers to see the pictures. In March 1996 another photographic evening was held with over forty generous villagers lending more than 400 pictures, creating an event that was of great interest both to long-time residents and newcomers. In 2003 an informal village history group was formed, meeting monthly in the Mure Hall, called Uplawmoor Local Studies Group.

This postcard showing a milk delivery in Uplawmoor is postmarked 2.30 p.m., 6 July 1906. William Carswell of Mid Uplaw Farm is thought to be the man holding the horse. He was one of seven sons. The high wall on the left surrounds the old village school, complete with its distinctive ventilation flèche. One of the neighbouring cottages housed Logan's sweetie shop and some customers can be seen outside it. The taller building on the right burned down in the 1920s.

Willie Rodger, who lived in Shillford, collected milk from local farms to deliver to the Co-operative Society in Shieldhall, Glasgow. This picture was taken when he won an annual competition for the best-kept milk lorry. It was an Albion and was one of the oldest on show that day.

Campbell and John Erskine photographed on the last day of their milk delivery, Saturday 27 April 1984. The Erskines of Mid Uplaw Farm had continued in the footsteps of the Frews and Carswells who had delivered milk to the village since the end of the nineteenth century. At one time the Raesides of Linnhead and the Borlands of South Uplaw Farm also brought milk – and probably butter and eggs – to the growing village. Originally milk was delivered by horse and cart and carried in churns, from which the farmer then filled jugs and pails belonging to villagers. When Bill Frew, father-in-law of John Erskine, delivered milk he would say: 'Straight to you, Frae the coo, Via Frew'! Milk from Uplawmoor was also delivered to the village of Lugton.

Glenhead Cottage originally belonged to the Caldwell Estate and may have dated from the early eighteenth century. At one time one of the rooms was used as a mission school, as shown on the Ainslie map of 1800. This 1982 photograph shows Willie Bates demolishing the cottage. His father, who, like him, was a builder, moved into Glenhead in 1920. Following its demolition a new house called Glenhead was built on this site in Tannoch Road next to the Mure Hall. The single gate at the side of the present-day house, which was saved during the demolition, dates from the time of the cottage's use as a school. Willie Bates's brother Thomas, who lived in the house opposite Mure Place, built Silverwood.

Shown here passing Caldwell Parish Church on Sunday 20 July 1983, the People's March for Jobs left from Glasgow as one of four feeder groups which formed the core of a march following the route of the Yarrow Hunger March of 1929. Danny Collins, Liboside councillor, was chief marshal, and funding was provided by the STUC and added to on the road by donations from the public, collected in buckets. Marchers were accommodated in community centres, church halls, a Sikh temple and other locations overnight, and were welcomed to Hyde Park by Ken Livingstone, then the leader of the Greater London Council and Mayor of London at the time of this book's preparation in 2004. The march promoted the issue of unemployment in difficult economic times. In London Danny Collins was kicked unconscious in an unprovoked attack by three members of the Workers' Revolutionary Party, but signed himself out of hospital in time to address the gathering in Hyde Park. His attackers faced the full force of the law at a later date.

The combined 'Fruit Basket' and post office at the corner of Tannoch Road and Neilston Road, photographed in 1985 when the pillar box was mysteriously painted white overnight. The event caused quite a stir, leading to police and CID arriving in the village, as defacing a pillar box is a Crown offence. The deed was attributed to high spirits by young people, no culprit was found, and unlike other youthful escapades time has not divulged the names of the villains. About the same time another fairly harmless happening occurred – one night almost all the garden gates in Neilston Road were removed from their posts and reinstalled one garden away, causing some alarm before their owners put them back in the right places.